First published in 1976 by
JUPITER BOOKS (LONDON) LIMITED
167 Hermitage Road, London N4 1LZ

SBN 904041 514



Composed on the Monophoto in 16/20pt Bembo 270
by Art Reprographic (London) Limited, London
Printed in Great Britain by
C. J. Mason and Sons Limited, Bristol.

# The Woolly Rhino
## FINDS A NEW HOME

Annabel Ogilvie *wrote the story*

T. A. B. Renton *drew the pictures*

JUPITER BOOKS

HE WOOLLY RHINO LAY happily relaxing under one of his favourite trees. 'What a beautiful day it is! A gentle sun to keep me warm, juicy grass to munch, open spaces to stroll in – who could ask for more?' 'I could,' said Fly, who was leaning against the Woolly Rhino's horn and looking a little miserable. 'Why, Fly,' said the Woolly Rhino, 'whatever is the matter?' 'Oh! for a space to rest my weary wings,' murmured Fly wistfully. The Woolly Rhino looked around at the rolling plains and said, rather tactlessly, that he thought there was plenty of space, and certainly enough to spare for a tiny Fly. 'I mean a home,' Fly said impatiently, 'a little place to call our own. Somewhere we can be snug and cosy.' 'What in the world do you want a home for?' demanded the Woolly Rhino. 'I'm quite content to stomp through the swamps and play under the trees! A home indeed!'

'Oh! do be quiet,' Fly said. 'I can hardly hear myself buzzing!'

The Woolly Rhino thought that he had, perhaps, been a little too harsh with Fly. After all, a home is not really too much to ask for, is it? He was a kindly soul and decided there and then that Fly would have a home and they would begin looking for it without delay.

This cheered Fly up considerably, and she even embraced the Woolly Rhino's horn gratefully with her tiny arms.

'Yes, let's!' Fly shouted, 'I'm sure we'll find a cosy cave or something! I'm sure we will!'

Feeling adventurous and brave the Woolly Rhino set off with Fly who, far too excited to perch on his horn as usual, buzzed happily to and fro around his head.

After they had jogged briskly along for a couple of miles they came to a gently sloping hill, in the side of which was a deep and dark hole surrounded by stately sunflowers, and bushes with such juicy-looking leaves that the Woolly Rhino's mouth began to water immediately.

'What a lovely place!' cried Fly enthusiastically. 'I'd be so very, very happy living in a place like this.'

The Woolly Rhino, who was by now hungry, edged closer to the cave mouth with the decided intention of sampling his future vegetable patch. His teeth were just about to close over a particularly tasty-looking leaf when a terrifying roar caused him to jump several feet into the air, roll over backwards and come to a shaky halt some distance away.

In the mouth of the cave stood a huge, handsome and most ferocious Sabre-Toothed Tiger. His great yellow eyes were fixed on them with an anything-but-friendly look . . .

'Grrrrr! What do you two think you're doing in my front garden? Grrrrrr! Tell me that!'

'I'm terribly sorry, Sir,' said the Woolly Rhino to the Tiger. 'We were just admiring your beautiful home . . .' But it was doubtful that the Tiger heard what he was saying – the Woolly Rhino's knees were knocking together and making a good deal of noise.

The Tiger bared his teeth and gave a blood-curdling roar.

'If you weren't so small I'd . . . I'd eat you both! For a snack – before dinner! On your way! Quickly, before I change my mind!' roared the Tiger.

Fly and the Woolly Rhino needed no further prompting, and they made off as fast as they could.

'And don't come back,' added the Tiger. 'Caves are for big, brave, beautiful, terrifying and toothy hunters like me! Little nuisances like you must find somewhere else to live.'

When Fly and the Woolly Rhino finally came to a halt after much puffing and panting, they found themselves in a wild and rocky valley littered with boulders.

'Well,' noted Fly, 'that seems to rule out nice cosy caves!'

'Never mind, Fly,' said the Woolly Rhino comfortingly. 'I never really had my heart set on a cave – let's leave them to horrid creatures like that Tiger.'

'This place seems rather nice,' observed Fly. 'There are lots of fine grasses for you to eat, and lovely flat rocks where I can lie and sunbathe. It only needs a few touches here and there to make it look quite homely.'

'I think we will have to do something about this rock,' said the Woolly Rhino kicking at a large brown boulder that lay nearby.

'That rock!' said Fly alarmed.

'What about it?'

'I'm almost sure it moved.'

'Don't be silly, Fly, rocks don't move. Well, certainly none of the rocks I've ever seen,' said the Woolly Rhino scornfully. And he promptly kicked the boulder again.

With quite amazing speed for something of its size the 'rock' rose to its feet and galloped off along the valley, shrieking indignantly.

'Now look what you have done,' said Fly. 'That was a baby Tyrannosaurus. And if you think it looked like a boulder, its mother will look like a mountain!'

Suddenly the sky above them darkened and a thunderous and threatening growl announced the approach of a Tyrannosaurus so huge that it filled the entire valley with its shadow.

'So!' said a deep and rumbling voice far above their heads, 'you think you can kick my baby and get away with it!'

'We're very sorry, really we are,' said Fly in her most humble voice as she flew from the Woolly Rhino's horn up towards the Tyrannosaurus. 'If we had realised that it was one of your lovely children we would *never* have touched him.'

'*Hmmmm*,' said the Tyrannosaurus, who was still very angry, but pleased to hear her child called 'lovely'. '*Hmmmm* – I think you'd better fly onto my nose and tell me what you are doing in my children's playground.'

Obediently Fly landed on the monstrous snout of the Tyrannosaurus where she appeared as a tiny pebble in a vast and empty desert.

'My friend and I,' Fly began, 'are looking for a home. We were nearly eaten by a Sabre-Toothed Tiger and we just stopped here for a rest before we continue on our way.'

'Hmmmm,' said the Tyrannosaurus again. 'Hmm – Hmm!'

Fly sat patiently on the Tyrannosaurus's nose while the monstrous towering creature slowly thought.

Meanwhile the Woolly Rhino was crouched on the ground far below, trying to outstare the baby Tyrannosaurus who was peering at him from behind its mother's tail.

'Valleys,' said the Tyrannosaurus at last, 'are for magnificent creatures like me. Little beasts like you must find somewhere else to live. On the other hand, I could give you to my children to play with . . .'

'Oh! Please don't do that,' pleaded Fly. 'We mean no harm.'

Despite her huge and terrifying size the Tyrannosaurus was really quite kindhearted and only meant to frighten them a little because they had kicked her baby.

'I'll count to ten,' she said, 'and if you are gone by the time I open my eyes, I will not give you to my children to play with.'

Greatly relieved, Fly flew down to the Woolly Rhino far below on the earth and explained what was happening.

'We best be off as fast as we can go,' responded the Woolly Rhino.

'Oh don't worry too much about that,' said Fly. 'I've never yet met a Tyrannosaurus who could count above three.'

Sure enough, as they walked over the hill and left the Tyrannosaurus in her valley, they could still hear her deep voice as she counted, 'One . . . one-and-a-quarter . . . three . . . eighteen . . . two-and-a-half . . .'

'Perhaps we'd better give up looking for a house,' the Woolly Rhino panted when they were quite beyond the domain of the Tyrannosaurus. 'It seems to be a very dangerous business.'

'Let's not stop just yet,' said Fly who, although she was exhausted, could not bear to give up the idea of her own home.

The Woolly Rhino, not wishing to disappoint her, agreed, and they set off once more – this time towards the misty blue mountains in the far distance.

When they did finally arrive at the foot of the mountains the Woolly Rhino's hooves were sore and tired and Fly had fallen asleep against his horn.

'Wake up,' said the Woolly Rhino, 'we're here! We've reached the misty mountains.'

Sleepily, Fly opened her eyes. There, all around, was lush green grass stretching along the foot of the mountains. A stream, after its heady descent down the mountain slopes, trickled lazily into a round blue lake.

'Woolly,' whispered Fly, 'this is perfect! I think we've found our home at last.'

But then, from far above, their peace was shattered by a blood-curdling scream which echoed around the rocks. They looked up towards the sun and squinted. There, perched high on a crag, was a shadowy figure.

'Oh no,' gasped the Woolly Rhino, 'it's a Pterodactyl!'

'I can see you!' hissed the menacing bird. 'I can see you very clearly from where I am.'

'I'm a Woolly Rhino,' explained the Woolly Rhino, 'and this is my friend Fly . . . who is a fly.'

'I'm in no mood for explanations,' said the Pterodactyl.

'And we're looking for a home,' continued the Woolly Rhino.

'This is my country here! Mountains are for Pterodactyls like me! And I'll show you what I do to people who come looking for homes here!'

Neither Fly nor the Woolly Rhino cared to debate this with the menacing bird because, with these words, the Pterodactyl swept off its crag and glided down towards them, hissing and screaming.

The Woolly Rhino quite forgot his aching hooves and, with Fly's panic-stricken squeaks to encourage him, ran off faster than his stubby legs had ever carried him.

'Quick, over there!' shouted Fly, pointing to a large hollow log which lay in their path. 'We can hide there until it goes away.'

No sooner were the words out of Fly's mouth than the Pterodactyl was swooping over their heads, missing them only by inches as they scuttled into the safety of the log.

But even as the menacing creature circled angrily over the log, hissing and cursing, the sky darkened and a low growl of thunder echoed around the mountains. Realising that a storm was threatening, the Pterodactyl turned towards the shelter of its nest. But suddenly a long silver finger of lightning raced downwards from behind a cloud – and the Pterodactyl's home crumbled into an untidy heap of boulders!

The Pterodactyl's scream was drowned in the rumbling laughter of the thunder, and the huge bird (quite forgetting about Fly and the Woolly Rhino) soared high into the air and raced quickly away to escape the fury of the storm.

From the safety of the log the Woolly Rhino watched the Pterodactyl depart.

'It's alright Fly,' said the Woolly Rhino turning around. 'It's gone. We can go home now.'

'Home?' muttered Fly, who was now stretching herself out most comfortably inside the spacious log. 'We have a roof over our heads, we are warm and dry and we have a pleasant view. Why, Woolly, I think this *is* home!'

'Thank goodness for that! I was getting rather bored house-hunting,' replied the Woolly Rhino.

'This just needs a few little touches . . .' said Fly, but when she turned to seek the Woolly Rhino's opinion he was curled up, fast asleep, in the doorway of their new home.